CALL to FAITH

KINDERGARTEN

Our Sunday Visitor

Curriculum Division

www.osvcurriculum.com

Nihil Obstat
Rev. Richard L. Schaefer

Imprimatur
✝ Most Rev. Thomas Wenski
Bishop of Orlando
December 14, 2007

The Imprimatur is an official declaration that a book or pamphlet is free of doctrinal or moral error. No implication is contained therein that anyone who granted the Imprimatur agrees with the contents, opinions, or statements expressed.

For permission to reprint copyrighted materials, grateful acknowledgment is made to the following sources:

Confraternity of Christian Doctrine, Washington, D.C.: Scriptures from the New American Bible. Text copyright © 1991, 1986, 1970 by the Confraternity of Christian Doctrine. All rights reserved. No part of the New American Bible may be used or reproduced in any form, without permission in writing from the copyright owner.

Hope Publishing Company, Carol Stream, IL 60188: Lyrics from "We Are the Church" by Richard K. Avery and Donald S. Marsh. Lyrics © 1972 by Hope Publishing Company.

The English translation of the Psalm Response from *Lectionary for Mass* © 1969, 1981, 1997, International Commission on English in the Liturgy Corporation (ICEL); excerpt from the English translation of *The Roman Missal* © 2010, ICEL. All rights reserved.

International Consultation on English Texts: English translation of Glory to the Father and Hail Mary by the International Consultation on English Texts.

OCP Publications, 5536 NE Hassalo, Portland, OR 97213: Lyrics from "Praise to You, O Christ, Our Savior" by Bernadette Farrell. Lyrics copyright © 1986 by Bernadette Farrell.

Printed in the United States of America

Call to Faith Kindergarten
ISBN: 978-0-15902-273-3
Item Number: CU1369

6 7 8 9 10 11 12 015016 15 14 13 12 11
Webcrafters, Inc., Madison, WI, USA; June 2011; Job# 92517

Kindergarten Contents

UNIT 1
REVELATION

© Our Sunday Visitor Curriculum Division

About You

You, O Lord, are good.
Based on Psalm 86:5

 **Let's Begin**

Welcome Kindergarten is an exciting grade. You will learn many new things. You will also get to know your teacher and your classmates.

Here is a way to help them get to know you.

Draw something you like to do.

1

About Your Faith

You will learn many things this year.

You will find out about the world God made. You will hear stories about God's Son, Jesus.

Your family at home and at church will help you.

Activity

Share Your Faith

Think: What is something you know about God?

Share: Talk about how you learned this.

Act: Work with your teacher to make a list of questions you have about God.

About Your Book

Your book has many things in it.

It has stories and pictures about God and his Son, Jesus.

It has prayers, songs, and activities, too.

Activity — Connect Your Faith

Seek and Find To get to know your book better, look at the pictures below. Then find an example of each picture somewhere in your book.

Call to Faith

Gather

Pray the Sign of the Cross together.

Leader: The Lord be with you.

All: And with your spirit.

Leader: Let us pray.

Bow your head as the leader prays.

All: Amen.

Listen to God's Word

Leader: A reading from the holy Gospel according to Matthew.

Read Matthew 4:18–22.

The Gospel of the Lord.

All: **Praise to you, Lord Jesus Christ.**

Signing of the Forehead

Come forward as your name is called. The leader will trace the Sign of the Cross on your forehead.

Leader: (Name), may God bless you as you answer Jesus' call to be his friend and follower.

All: Amen.

Go Forth!

Sing together.

We are called to act with justice,

we are called to love tenderly,

we are called to serve one another;

to walk humbly with God!

"We Are Called" © 1988, 2004 GIA Publications, Inc.

Special Times

Families share special times together. Some families celebrate birthdays and holidays with food, gifts, and songs.

The Church shares special times together, too. During the Church year, we celebrate the lives of Jesus, Mary, and the saints. We pray when we celebrate these special times. Here are three ways we pray.

We fold our hands in prayer.

We bow our heads in silence.

We make the Sign of the Cross.
We say,
In the name of the Father,
and of the Son,
and of the Holy Spirit. Amen.

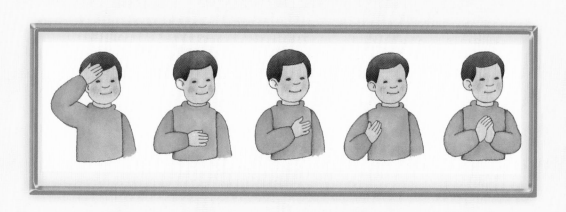

Our Mother

Mary was Jesus' mother.

She cared for him.

Mary cares for us, too.

We celebrate Mary's birthday on September 8.

Celebrate Mary

Gather

Sing together the refrain.

Ave, Ave, Ave Maria.

Ave, Ave, Maria.

"Immaculate Mary" © 1971, Faber Music, Ltd.

Pray the Sign of the Cross together.

Leader: The Lord be with you.

All: **And with your spirit.**

Leader: Let us pray.

Bow your heads as the leader prays.

All: **Amen.**

Listen to God's Word

Leader: A reading from the holy Gospel according to Luke.

Read Luke 1:46–48.

The Gospel of the Lord.

All: **Praise to you, Lord Jesus Christ.**

Go Forth!

Leader: Let us go forth to honor Mary.

All: **Thanks be to God.**

Jesus Is Coming!

Every year, we remember what life was like before Jesus was born.

We do this during a special time called Advent.

We wait for Jesus and get ready to see him again.

Celebrate Advent

Gather

Sing together the refrain.

Rejoice, Rejoice, Emmanuel

Shall come to you, O Israel.

"O Come, O Come Emmanuel" © 1975, GIA Publications, Inc.

Pray the Sign of the Cross together.

Leader: Blessed be God.

All: **Blessed be God forever.**

Leader: Let us pray.

Bow your heads as the leader prays.

All: **Amen.**

Listen to God's Word

Leader: A reading from the book of Isaiah.

Read Isaiah 40:3.

The word of the Lord.

All: **Thanks be to God.**

Go Forth!

Leader: Let us go to prepare our hearts for Jesus' birth.

All: **Thanks be to God.**

11

Jesus Comes

One dark night long ago, a baby was born.

The baby was Jesus.

Mary and Joseph welcomed him into their family.

We welcome Jesus into our family, too.

Celebrate Christmas

Gather

Sing together the refrain.

Go tell it on the mountain,

Over the hills and everywhere;

Go tell it on the mountain

That Jesus Christ is born.

"Go Tell It on the Mountain" © ND,
Mrs. John W. Work III

Pray the Sign of the Cross together.

Leader: Let us give thanks to God.

All: Let us give thanks to God.

Leader: Let us pray.

Bow your heads as the leader prays.

All: Amen.

Listen to God's Word

Leader: A reading from the holy Gospel according to Luke.

Read Luke 2:8–11.

The Gospel of the Lord.

All: Praise to you, Lord Jesus Christ.

Go Forth!

Leader: Let us share Jesus' love with others.

All: Thanks be to God.

13

Saint Francis of Assisi

Long ago, a young man lived in Italy. His name was Francis.

Francis loved plants and animals.

He loved people, too.

Most of all, Francis loved God.

Celebrate Creation

Gather

Sing together the refrain.

Sing out, earth and skies!

Sing of the God who loves you!

Raise your joyful cries!

Dance to the life around you!

"Sing Out, Earth and Skies" © 1985,
GIA Publications, Inc.

Pray the Sign of the Cross together.

Leader: Blessed be God.

All: **Blessed be God.**

Leader: Let us pray.

Bow your heads as the leader prays.

All: **Amen.**

Listen to God's Word

Leader: A reading from the book of Psalms.

Read Psalm 104:1, 24, 31.

The word of the Lord.

All: **Thanks be to God.**

Go Forth!

Leader: Let us go forth to enjoy the world.

All: **Thanks be to God.**

Changing Ourselves

Lent is a special time.

We try to change.

We try to grow in love.

We try to be more like Jesus.

Celebrate Lent

Gather

Sing together the refrain.

Lead me, guide me, along the way,

For if you lead me, I cannot stray.

Lord, let me walk each day with thee.

Lead me, oh Lord, lead me.

"Lead Me, Guide Me" © 1953, Doris M. Akers.
All rights administered by Unichapple Music, Inc.

Pray the Sign of the Cross together.

Leader: The Lord be with you.

All: And with your spirit.

Leader: Let us pray.

Bow your heads as the leader prays.

All: Amen.

Listen to God's Word

Leader: A reading from the holy Gospel according to Matthew.

Read Matthew 22:36–39.

The Gospel of the Lord.

All: Praise to you, Lord Jesus Christ.

Go Forth!

Leader: Let us grow in God's love.

All: Thanks be to God.

Holy Days

Holy Thursday, Good Friday, Holy Saturday, and Easter Sunday are special days.

They are the holiest days of the year.

On these days, we remember that Jesus loved us very much.

Celebrate Jesus

Gather

Sing together the refrain.

Jesus, remember me when you come into your Kingdom.

Jesus, remember me when you come into your Kingdom.

"Jesus, Remember Me" © 1981, Les Presses de Taizé, GIA Publications, Inc., agent

Pray the Sign of the Cross together.

Leader: The Lord be with you.

All: And with your spirit.

Leader: Let us pray.

Bow your heads as the leader prays.

All: Amen.

Listen to God's Word

Leader: A reading from the book of Philippians.

Read Philippians 2:8–11.

The word of the Lord.

All: Thanks be to God.

Go Forth!

Leader: Jesus has done great things for us.

All: Thanks be to God.

Jesus Is with Us!

Easter is a special day.

On Easter, we celebrate that Jesus was raised from the dead.

He had new life. He shares his life with us.

Celebrate Easter

Gather

Sing together the refrain.

Alleluia, alleluia, give thanks to the risen Lord.

Alleluia, alleluia, give praise to his Name.

"Alleluia, Alleluia, Give Thanks" © 1973, Word of God Music

Pray the Sign of the Cross together.

Leader: The Lord be with you, alleluia.

All: And with your spirit, alleluia.

Leader: Let us pray.

Bow your heads as the leader prays.

All: Amen.

Listen to God's Word

Leader: A reading from the Holy Gospel according to Matthew.

Read Matthew 28:5–7.

The Gospel of the Lord.

All: Praise to you, Lord Jesus Christ.

Go Forth!

Leader: Let us celebrate Jesus' new life.

All: Thanks be to God, alleluia.

The Holy Spirit

Jesus sent the Holy Spirit to us.

The Holy Spirit helps us make choices.

He guides you to follow Jesus.

On Pentecost, we celebrate that he is with us.

Celebrate Pentecost

Gather

Sing together the refrain.

Come Lord Jesus, send us your
Spirit, renew the face of the earth.

Come, Lord Jesus, send us your
Spirit, renew the face of the earth.

"Send Us Your Spirit" © 1981, 1982, 1987,
GIA Publications, Inc.

Pray the Sign of the Cross together.

Leader: Blessed be God.

All: **Blessed be God forever.**

Leader: Let us pray.

Bow your heads as the leader prays.

All: **Amen.**

Listen to God's Word

Leader: A reading from the Acts of
the Apostles.

Read Acts 2:1–4.

The Word of the Lord.

All: **Thanks be to God.**

Go Forth!

Leader: The Holy Spirit is with us today.

All: **Thanks be to God.**

CALL
to
FAITH
e connect

God Made the World

The earth is full of your creation.

Based on Psalm 104:24

 Read to Me

Let's Begin

God's Gift

Under the sun and moon,
In a sea of cool, clean air,
Floats the beautiful world
God made for us to share.

● Who shares the world with you?

God's World

The world and everything in it belongs to God.

Psalm 50:10–11

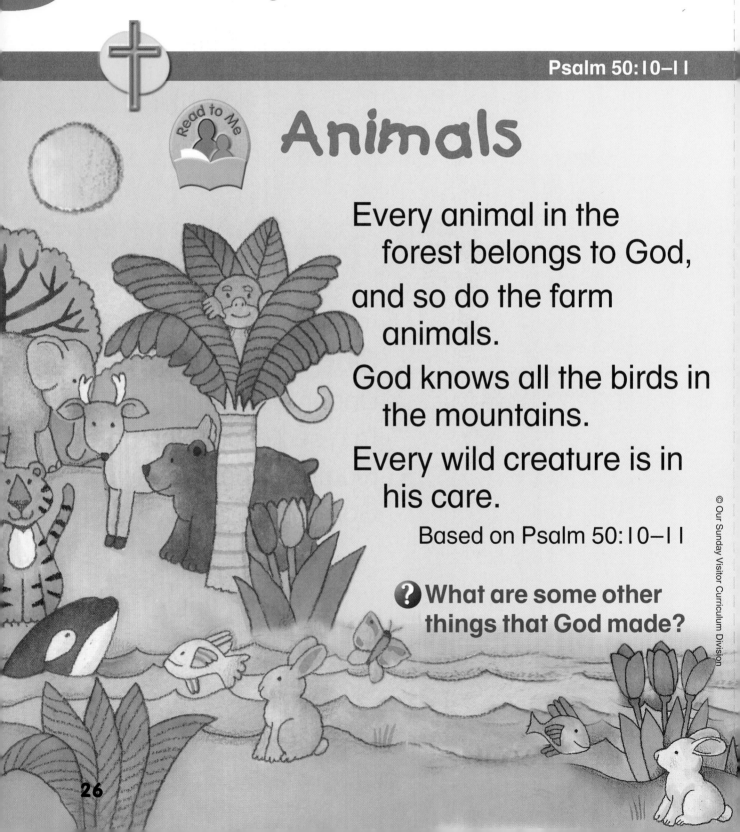

Read to Me

Animals

Every animal in the forest belongs to God,

and so do the farm animals.

God knows all the birds in the mountains.

Every wild creature is in his care.

Based on Psalm 50:10–11

? What are some other things that God made?

Care for the World

God wants us to take care of the things he made.

Activity

Tell how the people in the picture are caring for the world.

Litter

KEEP PARK CLEAN

Litter

Thank God

We thank God for the world
with prayers.

Animals thank God with sounds.

Activity

Pretend you are an animal and
use its sound to thank God.

 Bees thank God by buzzing.

 Birds thank God by tweeting.

 Cows thank God by mooing.

 Dogs thank God by barking.

 Lions thank God by roaring.

Prayer of Thanks

Think about the things that make you happy. Say a quiet prayer to thank God for one thing that makes you happy.

Sing together.

All things bright and beautiful,
All creatures great and small,
All things wise and wonderful,
The Lord God made them all.

All Things Bright and Beautiful

Family Faith

Catholics Believe

Dear Family,

In Chapter 1, the children learned that God made the world. We share the world with other creatures. We are meant to take care of the creatures in the world. All creatures of the world praise God.

✝ SCRIPTURE

Read Psalm 50:10–11 together with your child.

GO online **www.osvcurriculum.com**
For weekly scripture readings and seasonal resources

Family Project

God Made Our World Take a family trip to a local zoo, park, or public garden. With your child, note the variety of birds, animals, and plants that God created. Talk about how each one is special. With your child, say a prayer thanking God for creation.

ZOO
Birds
Reptiles
Polar Bears

People of Faith

Each day Catherine thanked God for giving her the things of the earth.

Saint Catherine ▶ of Siena, 1347–1380

 Family Prayer

Gracious God, help us be like Saint Catherine. Help us thank you every day for the gift of creation. Amen.

CCC See Catechism of the Catholic Church 339, 358 for further reading on chapter content.

God Made You

 I praise you for making me so wonderfully.

Based on Psalm 139:14

 Read to Me — **Let's Begin**

What Do You See?

You look in the mirror,
and what do you see?
Two big eyes staring at me.

You look in the mirror,
and what do you see?
A shiny nose pointing at me.

You look in the mirror,
and what do you see?
Two ruby lips smiling at me.

● What else do you see
in the mirror?

31

Made With Love

God made all people on earth!

You are special because God made you.

Genesis 1:27–28

Like God

God made you to be like him.
He made boys and girls.
God blessed you and all people.

Based on Genesis 1:27–28

 How does God bless you?

You Are Special

Each person is different.

Each person is special.

Activity

Look at the circle on this page.

Make the person in the circle look like you.

Our Special Gifts

The way we look is not the only special thing about us.

Things we do are special, too.

Activity

What can you do that is special?

Act out one of the special things you do.

Thank You, God!

Leader: Thank you, God, for making us like you.

All: **Thank you, God, for making us like you.**

Leader: Thank you, God, for helping us do special things.

All: **Thank you, God, for helping us do special things.**

Sing together.

All things bright and beautiful,
All creatures great and small,
All things wise and wonderful,
The Lord God made them all.

All Things Bright and Beautiful

Family Faith

Catholics Believe

Dear Family,

In Chapter 2, the children learned that God made all people on the earth. They learned that each person is different from everyone else. They also shared their special talents with each other.

✝ SCRIPTURE

Read Genesis 1:27–28 together with your child.

GO online www.osvcurriculum.com
For weekly scripture readings and seasonal resources

Family Project

Our Special Family Make a place mat that will remind you of friends and family members who live far away. Glue pictures of the people onto a sheet of construction paper. Label the collage "Our Special Family." After the glue dries, cover the collage with clear adhesive paper. Use the finished place mat during family meals.

Our Special Family

People of Faith

Catherine knew that she was special. God made her just like him.

Saint Catherine ▶ of Siena, 1347–1380

Family Prayer

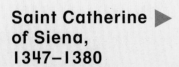

God our Father, help us see you in ourselves. Help us know that we are like you. Amen.

CCC *See Catechism of the Catholic Church 356 for further reading on chapter content.*

Chapter 3

God Loves You

Your love for me is great.

Based on Psalm 86:13

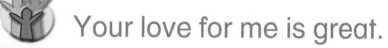 Read to Me

Let's Begin

Showing Love

We show love to others in our kindergarten class.

Antonio helps Benjamin with his coat.

Charles shares a snack with Devon.

Frances paints a picture for Ricky.

George gives a crayon to Harriet.

● How do you show love to others in your class?

37

God's Love

God showed love by making everyone on earth.

God loves everyone.

I Corinthians 13:4

What Is Love?

Love is being kind to others.
Love is being patient with each other.

Based on I Corinthians 13:4

❓ **Why do kindness and patience show love?**

Show Love

You show love when you smile at others. Other people show love when they smile at you.

You show love when you wait for others. Others show love when they wait for you.

Activity

Draw a heart around each picture that shows love.

39

Learn About God's Love

God's love is all around us.

We learn about God's love through our senses.

Our senses are gifts from God.

Activity

 Draw a line to connect each sense with what it tells us about.

Prayer of Love

Leader: God teaches us about his love.

All: **We love you, God.**

Leader: God helps us show love to others.

All: **We love you, God.**

Sing together.

All things bright and beautiful,

All creatures great and small,

All things wise and wonderful,

The Lord God made them all.

All Things Bright and Beautiful

41

Catholics Believe

Dear Family,

In Chapter 3, the children learned about God's love for us. They learned that God wants us to show love to other people. They found that their senses tell them about God's love for them.

SCRIPTURE

Read I Corinthians 13:4 together with your child.

GO online www.osvcurriculum.com
For weekly scripture readings and seasonal resources

Family Project

Loving Others Encourage your child to practice acts of kindness. Talk with him or her about how acts of kindness show love. Challenge your child to perform at least one act of kindness each day. Label a sheet of paper "Loving Others" and help your child list the kind acts he or she does each day. At the end of a week, review the list and praise his or her successes.

Loving Others

People of Faith

Catherine knew that God loved her. She wrote about God's love for her and for others. People still read her book today.

Saint Catherine ▶ of Siena, 1347–1380

Family Prayer

Saint Catherine, help us remember that God loves us. Help us teach one another about God's love. Amen.

© Our Sunday Visitor Curriculum Division

Scripture Story

God Made All Things

(Genesis 1:1–2:4)

Family Note: In class your child has learned that God made all things. Read this Scripture Story together. Then have your child use all the pictures to retell the story. Tell your child that you are happy God has created him or her!

And God made people just like you.

Draw yourself.

8

43

God made the day.
God said, "Let there be light."

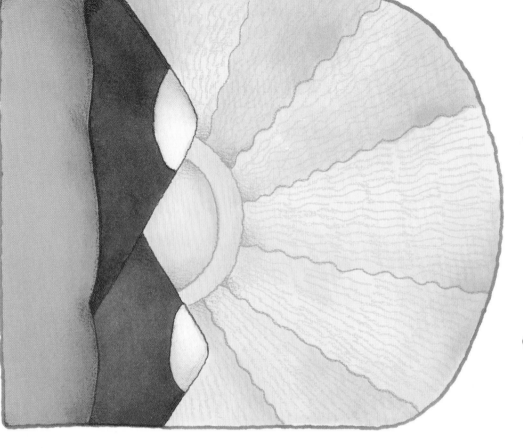

2

Draw plants and animals.

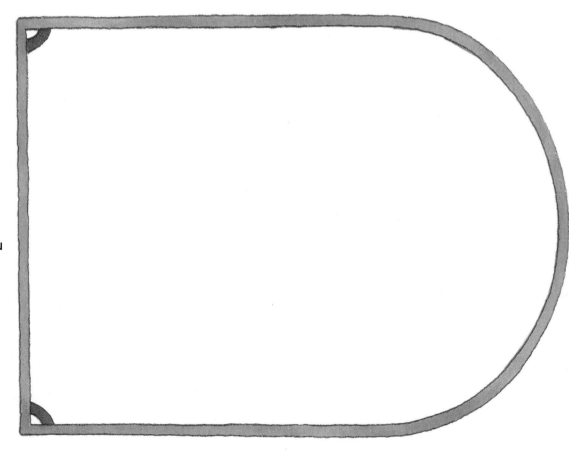

7

Draw the sun.

3

God made the plants.

God made the animals, too.

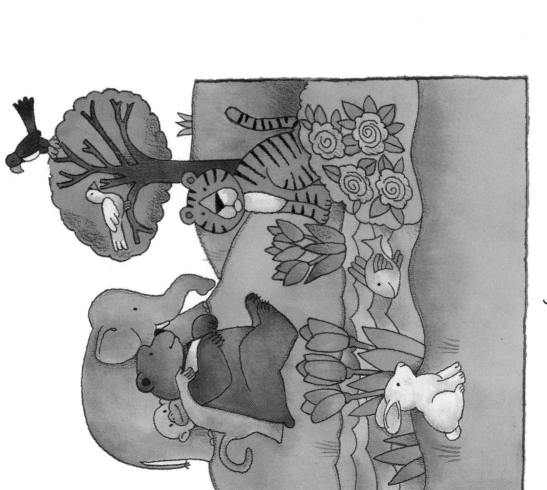

6

45

God made the night.
God made the moon and stars
so bright.

4

Draw the moon and stars.

5

46

Chapter 4 God the Father

 God said, "You are my child. I am your father."

Based on Psalm 2:7

Let's Begin

Learn About God's Love

Mr. Rillon's class drew pictures of special people.

- Carlos and his mother plant roses.

- Ivana and her aunt work in the garden.

- Braulio and his dad cook.

- Jean's grandfather reads to her.

What wonderful things have you learned from special people?

Special People

Moms, dads, grandmas, grandpas, aunts, and uncles are all special.

They love you and teach you many things.

Activity

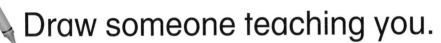 Draw someone teaching you.

God Shows Love

God shows love by giving us people who love us. He shows his love in other ways, too.

I John 3:1

Child of God

See what love God the Father gives you.

You are a child of God because he loves you.

Based on I John 3:1

? How does God love you?

49

God the Father

Everyone is a child of God.

Everyone belongs to God.

God is our Father.

Activity

Match each picture with the best words.

People who love
us help us.

People who love
us forgive us.

People who love
us teach us.

I Believe

Leader: God made everything.

All: **I believe in God the Father.**

Leader: God loves us very much.

All: **I believe in God the Father.**

Leader: God takes care of us.

All: **I believe in God the Father.**

Sing together the refrain.

All grownups, all children,
all mothers, all fathers are
sisters and brothers
in the fam'ly of God.

All Grownups, All Children

Family Faith

Catholics Believe

Dear Family,

In Chapter 4, the children learned that God is the Father of us all. Children may not understand this because we cannot see God. Children learn about God's love from your example.

SCRIPTURE

Read 1 John 3:1 together with your child.

GO online www.osvcurriculum.com
For weekly scripture readings and seasonal resources

Family Project

Start a Love Note Jar Wash and decorate a jar. As you observe family members showing love for one another, write down what you see and the family member's name. For example, "Ben held the door for a person at church." Place the paper in the jar. Collect papers for a week or so. At a family meal, read aloud the papers. Praise the loving actions, and encourage family members to continue the good work.

People of Faith

Saint Pier Giorgio Frassati lived in Italy. As a young man he went to Mass every day.

Saint Pier Giorgio Frassati, ▶ 1901–1925

Family Prayer

Pier, pray for us, that we may worship God as you did. Amen.

© Our Sunday Visitor Curriculum Division

Chapter 5 You Pray

To you I pray, O LORD.

Based on Psalm 5:3

Read to Me — Let's Begin

Talking with Grandmother

Emily called her grandmother and said, "Good morning, Grandma!"

After school, Emily called her grandmother and said, "I learned to read two new words today!"

At bedtime, Emily called her grandmother and said, "Good night. I love you, Grandma!"

Grandma said, "I love you, too. Thanks for sharing your day with me."

● Why did Emily call her grandmother so often?

Talking with God

Emily's grandmother loves her. She loves it when Emily calls her.

God loves you. He wants you to talk to him. You talk to him when you pray.

I Thessalonians 5:17–18

Read to Me

Pray Always

One of God's followers told us when to pray. Pray all the time to God. Thank God for everything that happens.

Based on
I Thessalonians 5:17–18

❓ **When can you pray to God?**

© Our Sunday Visitor Curriculum Division

54

Ways to Pray

Pray to God in your heart with your own words.

● Pray to God when you are happy.

● Pray to God when someone is sick.

● Pray to God when you feel lonely.

? **What do you say when you pray?**

We Believe

We believe in God the Father.
We believe in Jesus, God's Son.
We believe in God the Holy Spirit.

Activity

Make a sign that will remind you to pray.

The Sign of the Cross

 We begin and end our prayers with the Sign of the Cross.

In the name of the Father,

1

and of the Son,

2

and of the Holy Spirit.

3

4

Amen.

5

 Sing together.

All grownups, all children,
all mothers, all fathers are
sisters and brothers
in the fam'ly of God.

All Grownups, All Children

Catholics Believe

Dear Family,
In Chapter 5, the children learned that praying is talking to God. They learned to make the Sign of the Cross to begin and end prayers.

SCRIPTURE

Read 1 Thessalonians 5:17–18 together with your child.

GO online www.osvcurriculum.com
For weekly scripture readings and seasonal resources

Family Project

Pray for Others
Make a list of people you want to remember in your family prayers. Have your child decorate the list. Post the list where you can read the names as part of mealtime or evening prayers. Add to the list as needed. Remind your child to begin and end prayers with the Sign of the Cross.

Prayer List
mother
father
Lucca
Beth

People of Faith

Saint Pier Giorgio Frassati liked to ski. He also liked to climb mountains. Pier was cheerful, even when he was sick.

Saint Pier Giorgio Frassati, ▶ 1901–1925

Family Prayer

Almighty God, help us be like Pier Frassati. Help us to be strong when we are sick or sad. Amen.

Chapter 6

You Care

Let all who live in God's world care for it.

Based on Psalm 33:8

Read to Me

Let's Begin

Hurt No Living Thing

Hurt no living thing:
Ladybird, nor butterfly,
Nor moth with dusty wing,
Nor cricket chirping cheerily,
Nor grasshopper so light
  of leap,
Nor dancing gnat, nor
  beetle fat,
Nor harmless worms
  that creep.

by Christina Rossetti

● What living things
do you care for?

God's World

God loves all living things.

When you care for the earth,
you show your love for God.

Genesis 1:28

Read to Me Take Care

God told the first people to take
care of the fish in the sea, the
birds in the air, and all living things.

Based on Genesis 1:28

? How do people take care of
God's creation?

Ways to Care

You are old enough to help care for God's world.

Throw trash into the trash can.

Use water wisely.

Put things where they belong.

Activity

Tell how the people in each picture are caring for God's world. Draw a way you can care for God's world.

Protect God's World

This song will remind you to care for creation.

Activity

Work with a partner. Add one line to the song. Sing the line to the class.

Sing together.

This is the way we protect God's world, so early in the morning.
This is the way we pick up trash, so early in the morning.
This is the way we water God's plants, so early in the morning.
This is the way we save our water, so early in the morning.

Pray with God's Word

Leader: Let us listen to God's word.

Read Genesis 1:27–28.

The word of the Lord.

All: Thanks be to God.

 Sing together.

All grownups, all children,
all mothers, all fathers are
sisters and brothers
in the fam'ly of God.

All Grownups, All Children

 Catholics Believe

Dear Family,

In Chapter 6, the children learned that people are responsible for caring for plants, animals, and other people. The children learned that they can help care for creation, too.

 **SCRIPTURE**

Read Genesis 1:28 together with your child.

GO online www.osvcurriculum.com
For weekly scripture readings and seasonal resources

Family Project

Care for the Earth Discuss how recycling helps save the earth's resources. Participate in a community recycling program. Encourage your child to help you stack newspapers, place cans and bottles in the proper containers, and so on. Point out that these efforts help care for the earth and keep your home and community clean.

People of Faith

Saint Pier Giorgio Frassati tried to make other people happy. He lived his faith at home and at school. He cared for poor people each day.

Saint Pier Giorgio Frassati, ▶ 1901–1925

 Family Prayer

God our Father, help us be like Pier Frassati. Teach us to help the poor. Amen.

Scripture Story
Noah's Ark
(Genesis 6–9)

Family Note: In class your child has learned that God is a loving Father. As you read aloud this booklet, have your child use the pictures to follow along. Then have him or her tell you the story of how God helped Noah.

God promised Noah that water would never again flood the whole earth. God said, "A rainbow is a sign of my promise." Color the rainbow.

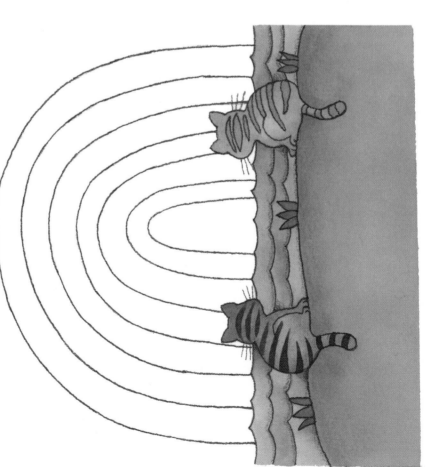

8

65

Long, long ago, God told Noah that there would be a flood. "Build a big boat," said God. So Noah built an ark.

2

© Our Sunday Visitor Curriculum Division

Then the rain stopped. The sun came out. The water dried up slowly. Noah's family and all the animals left the ark.

7

God said, "Take animals with you, Noah. Get two of every kind."

3

It rained for forty days and forty nights. The water rose higher and higher. Finally, water flooded the whole earth.

6

Noah led the animals into the ark two by two.

4

5

Chapter 7 God Sends His Son

 You are my Son.

Based on Psalm 2:7

Read to Me — Let's Begin

Helping

The phone rang.

My dad said proudly, "Yes, my son can help you. He can take in your mail, Mrs. Posey."

Dad said, "Ramon, our neighbor needs you."

"I can help, Dad," I said. "You can send your son."

Dad smiled and hugged me.

● Why was Dad proud to send Ramon to help?

God's Son

Dad knew that Ramon could help Mrs. Posey.

God the Father knew that his people needed help. He sent his Son to help. Jesus is God's Son.

We celebrate Jesus' birth on Christmas.

Activity

Draw baby Jesus with Mary and Joseph.

Read to Me

Jesus Is Born

Joseph and Mary went to Bethlehem.
Clip, clop marched the donkey.

Joseph went to the inn, but there were no empty rooms.
"No rooms, no rooms," Joseph said.

Joseph and Mary went to sleep in the stable.
"Good night, good night," said the animals.

Mary's baby was born.
"Sweet baby, sweet baby," Mary said.

Joseph and Mary named the baby Jesus.

We are glad you are here, dear Jesus.

Based on Luke 2:1-7

❓ **Who took care of God's Son?**

Who Knew?

Mary and Joseph knew that Jesus was God's Son.

They knew that Jesus would help God's people.

Soon many people learned that Jesus was God's Son.

Activity

Number the pictures to tell the story of Jesus' birth. Then color the pictures.

Prayer of Praise

Leader: We love Jesus.

All: **We love Jesus.**

Leader: We want to be like him.

All: **We want to be like him. Amen.**

Sing together.

Praise to you, O Christ, Our Savior,
Word of the Father, calling us to life;
Son of God, who leads us to freedom:
Glory to you, Lord Jesus Christ.

Praise to You, O Christ, Our Savior

Catholics Believe

Dear Family,

In Chapter 7, the children learned that Jesus is God's Son. God sent Jesus to help his people. Mary is Jesus' mother. Joseph watched over Jesus and Mary.

✝ SCRIPTURE

Read Luke 2:1–7 together with your child.

GO online www.osvcurriculum.com
For weekly scripture readings and seasonal resources

Family Project

Acting Like Jesus Point out that Jesus helped Mary and Joseph at home. This week, pick out several jobs that your child can help you with. As you work, praise your child's efforts. Mention that your child is imitating Jesus by helping you.

People of Faith

Simeon was an old man at the time of Jesus' birth. He prayed every day for God to send someone to help God's people.

Holy Simeon, ▶
ca. 66B.C.–3A.D.

Family Prayer

God the Father, thank you for people like Simeon who give us a good example of prayer. Amen.

© Our Sunday Visitor Curriculum Division

Jesus Teaches

 Teach me your paths.
Based on Psalm 25:4

Let's Begin

Many Teachers

You have many teachers in your life.

Teachers share things they know.

Teachers show you how to do things.

Teachers help you learn.

● When have you been like a teacher?

About Jesus

The Bible is the Church's holy book. It tells you about Jesus.

Activity

What was Jesus doing in each of these pictures?

• Jesus prayed.

• Jesus healed sick people.

• Jesus fed hungry people.

• Jesus told stories.

Asking Prayer

Leader: Jesus, teach us to love everyone.

All: **Jesus, teach us to love everyone.**

Leader: Teach us to be kind.

All: **Teach us to be kind. Amen.**

Sing together.

Praise to you, O Christ,
  Our Savior,
Word of the Father,
  calling us to life;
Son of God who
  leads us to freedom:
Glory to you,
  Lord Jesus Christ.

Praise to You, O Christ,
Our Savior

Family Faith

Catholics Believe

Dear Family,

In Chapter 8, the children learned that Jesus is a great teacher. He teaches all of us to love and to be kind. Most of all, Jesus teaches us to be like God the Father.

✝ SCRIPTURE

Read Luke 6:27–36 together with your child.

GO online **www.osvcurriculum.com**
For weekly scripture readings and seasonal resources

Family Project

Be a Teacher Like Jesus Set up a play date with a younger child. Invite your child to teach this younger friend a game or a new skill. Work with the children to assure that all goes well. Praise both children for their success in working together.

People of Faith

Mary and Joseph took baby Jesus to the Temple. Simeon recognized that Jesus was sent by God.

Holy Simeon, ▶
ca. 66 B.C.–3 A.D.

Family Prayer
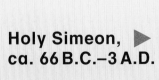

Loving God, help us be like Simeon. Help us recognize Jesus. Keep us in his love. Amen.

Chapter 9 You Follow Jesus

 You will show me the path to life.

Based on Psalm 16:11

Let's Begin

Follow the Leader

It was playtime.

Mrs. Harper taught the children a game.

One child was the leader.

Everyone followed what the leader did.

Play this game with your class.

● What were some things your class leader did?

Jesus the Leader

Jesus leads you to be kind.

He leads you to obey.

He leads you to pray.

You are a follower of Jesus.

Activity

Draw a line from Jesus to the people who are following him.

Following Jesus

The Bible tells many stories about Jesus and his followers.

Mark 1:16–19

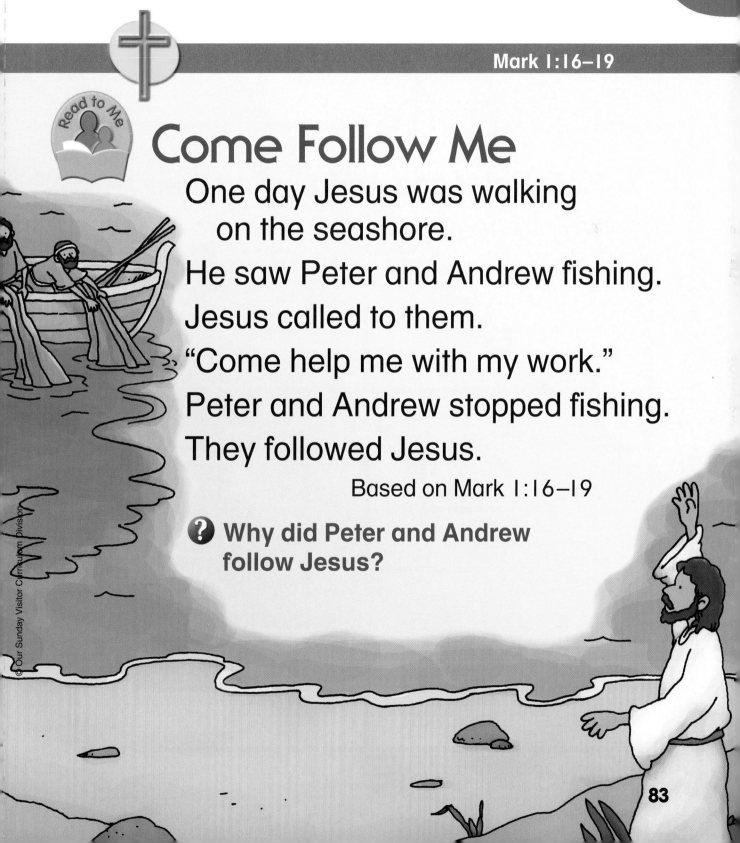

Read to Me

Come Follow Me

One day Jesus was walking
on the seashore.

He saw Peter and Andrew fishing.

Jesus called to them.

"Come help me with my work."

Peter and Andrew stopped fishing.

They followed Jesus.

Based on Mark 1:16–19

❓ **Why did Peter and Andrew follow Jesus?**

83

Jesus' Followers

Jesus has many followers.
Jesus' followers are called Christians.
You are a Christian.

Activity

Help Peter and Andrew find their way to Jesus.

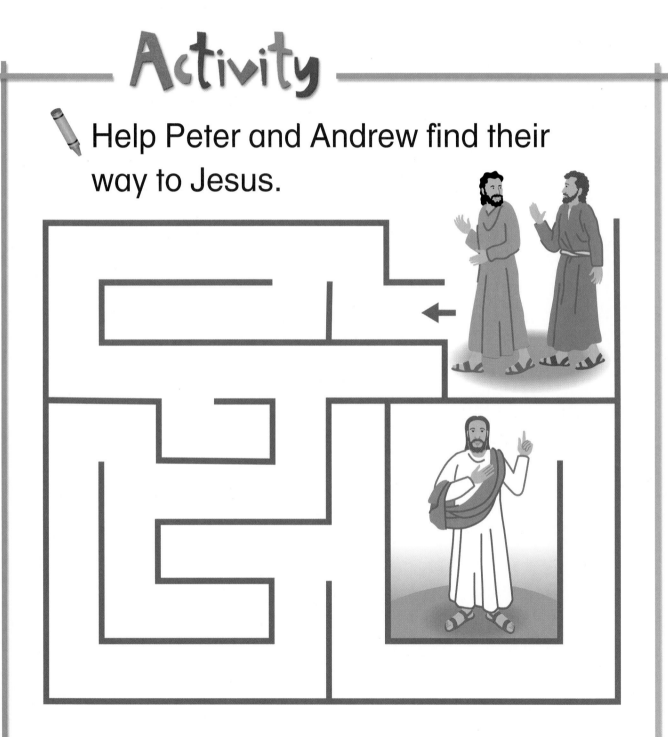

Prayer for Help

Leader: Jesus, thank you for being
our leader.
Help us be like Andrew and Peter.
Help us hear you calling.
Help us follow you and learn
from you.
Help us be good Christians.

All: **Amen.**

Sing together.

Praise to you, O Christ,
  Our Savior,
Word of the Father,
  calling us to life;
Son of God who leads
  us to freedom:
Glory to you,
  Lord Jesus Christ.

Praise to You, O Christ,
Our Savior

 ## Catholics Believe

Dear Family,
In Chapter 9, the children learned that Jesus asks us to follow him. The children heard the story of Jesus calling Peter and Andrew. They learned that followers of Jesus are called Christians.

 ## SCRIPTURE

Read Mark 1:16–19 together with your child.

GO online **www.osvcurriculum.com**
For weekly scripture readings and seasonal resources

Family Project

Follow the Leader Take turns being leaders and followers. Choose several different activities, such as chores, recreational pastimes, and prayer. Talk with your child about the responsibilities of being a leader. During a family prayer time, pray for the leaders of the parish, community, and country.

People of Faith

Simeon knew Jesus would be a great teacher. Simeon praised God and thanked him for Jesus.

Holy Simeon, ▶
ca. 66 B.C.–3 A.D.

 ## Family Prayer

Gracious God, we praise you. We thank you for sending Jesus to lead us. Amen.

Scripture Story

The Good Neighbor

(Luke 10:25–37)

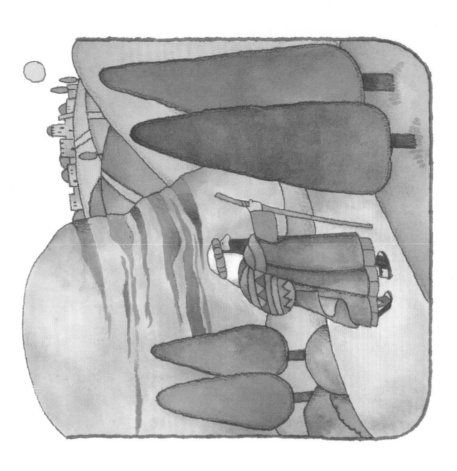

Jesus said, "Be like the good man. Love your neighbor." Color the heart.

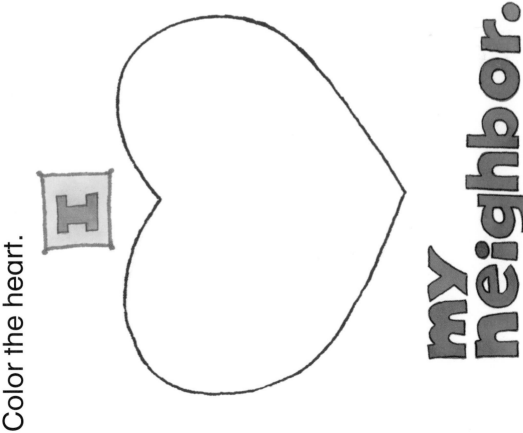

my **neighbor.**

8

Family Note: In class your child has learned that Jesus taught us to love each other. Read this Scripture Story together. It is the story of the Good Samaritan, a man who loved his neighbor. Ask your child to tell you what the Good Samaritan did.

Long ago, a man asked Jesus,
"How can I be a good neighbor?"

2

Finally, a third man came by.
He stopped and helped.
He was a good man.

7

Jesus answered him by telling a story.

Once upon a time, a man was traveling to town.

3

Then, a second man walked by. He did not stop to help either.

6

All of a sudden, some men robbed the man and beat him up!

The man was hurt and needed help.

A little while later, a man walked by.

He did not stop to help.

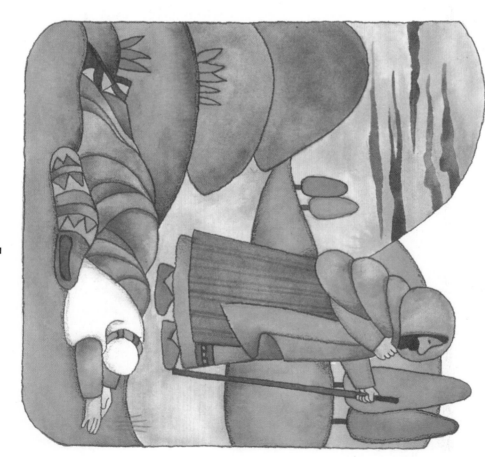

The Church

I want to pray in the Lord's house all the days of my life.

Based on Psalm 27:4

Read to Me

Let's Begin

The Church

Here is the church.
Here is the steeple.
Open the doors,
And see all the people.

● Name some people you see in your Church.

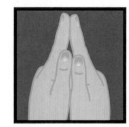
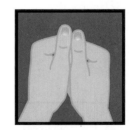

Church Family

The people in the Church are like a family.

Each Sunday your Church family prays together.

Colossians 3:15–17

How We Live

Church family members should love each other.
You should pray and sing to God.
You should thank God.

Based on Colossians 3:15–17

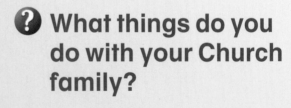 **What things do you do with your Church family?**

All Are Welcome

People of different ages are part of the Church.

People of different colors are part of the Church, too.

Everyone is welcome in the Church.

Activity

Draw your Church family.

The Church Follows Jesus

Every day, the Church family follows Jesus.

The Church family does what Jesus said to do.

The Church family shows God's love for everyone.

Activity

Tell how each picture shows the Church family following Jesus.

Prayer for Others

Leader: Loving God, thank you for the people in our Church family.

All: **Thank you for the people in our Church family.**

Leader: They help us follow Jesus.

All: **They help us follow Jesus.**

Leader: They help us show your love.

All: **They help us show your love. Amen.**

Sing together.

I am the Church!
   You are the Church!
We are the Church
   together.
All who follow Jesus,
   all around the world!
Yes, we're the Church
   together.

We Are the Church

95

CHAPTER 12

Family Faith

Catholics Believe

Dear Family,

In Chapter 10, the children learned that they belong to a Church family. The Church family is made up of people of all races and ages. The Church family meets to pray and sing to God. The Church family follows Jesus.

✝ SCRIPTURE

Read Colossians 3:15–17 together with your child.

GO online **www.osvcurriculum.com**
For weekly scripture readings and seasonal resources

Family Project

The Church Family Participate as a family in a parish activity, such as a dinner, group outing, or community service project. By doing so, you show that you are part of a bigger family—the Church family. After the event, talk with your child about the Church members you met and how they worked together and enjoyed each other's company.

People of Faith

Saint Philip was a special follower of Jesus. He was one of Jesus' first followers.

Saint Philip ▶ the Apostle, first century

Family Prayer

God our Father, help us be special followers of Jesus. Help us be good members of the Church family.

CCC *See Catechism of the Catholic Church 751, 752 for further reading on chapter content.*

The Holy Spirit

 You guide me along the right path.

Based on Psalm 23:3

 Read to Me — **Let's Begin** —

Who Has Seen the Wind?

Who has seen the wind?
Neither I nor you:
But when the leaves hang
    trembling,
The wind is passing through.
Who has seen the wind?
Neither you nor I:
But when the trees bow
    down their heads,
The wind is passing by.

by Christina Rossetti

● How do you know the
    wind is near you?

97

The Spirit Comes

Some of Jesus' friends were praying together.

Suddenly, there was a noise like a strong wind.

Jesus' friends were filled with the Holy Spirit.

The Holy Spirit helped the friends teach many people about Jesus.

Based on Acts 2:1–4

? **How did Jesus' friends know that the Holy Spirit had come?**

A Helper

The Holy Spirit came like the wind to the Church.

Jesus sent the Holy Spirit to be with his friends.

He helps the Church family follow Jesus.

He guides the Church.

Activity

How is the Holy Spirit guiding the people in the pictures?

The Holy Trinity

There are three Persons in God.

God the Father made us.

God the Son is Jesus. He teaches us.

God the Holy Spirit helps God's people.

God the Father, God the Son, and God the Holy Spirit together are the Holy Trinity.

Activity

These circles remind you of the Holy Trinity.

Color each circle.

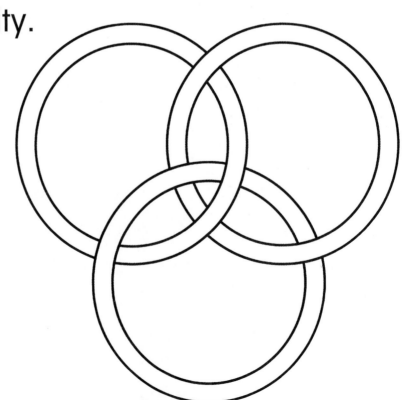

Helping Prayer

Leader: Holy Spirit, Jesus sent you to his friends. You helped them do God's work. Please come to us now. Help us be friends to Jesus. Help us do God the Father's work. Thank you.

All: Amen.

Sing together.

I am the Church! You are
 the Church!
We are the Church
 together.
All who follow Jesus,
 all around the world!
Yes, we're the
 Church together.

We Are the Church

Chapter 11 — Family Faith

Catholics Believe

Dear Family,

In Chapter 11, the children learned about the Holy Spirit. The Holy Spirit guides the Church family. They learned that the Holy Spirit is God. God the Father, Jesus, and the Holy Spirit make up the Holy Trinity.

✝ SCRIPTURE

Read Acts 2:1–4 together with your child.

GO online www.osvcurriculum.com
For weekly scripture readings and seasonal resources

Family Project

The Holy Spirit As a reminder that the Holy Spirit is with your family, make or buy a wind sock or wind chimes. Tell family members that they cannot see the wind, but they can see and hear it working. Point out that the Holy Spirit is like the wind. We cannot see him, but we can see the results of his work in the world. Suggest that family members say a prayer to the Holy Spirit whenever they hear the chimes or see the wind sock move.

People of Faith

Saint Philip was among Jesus' friends when the Holy Spirit came like the wind.

Saint Philip ▶ the Apostle, first Century

Family Prayer

Come Holy Spirit, fill our hearts with your love. Help us serve God and others. Amen.

© Our Sunday Visitor Curriculum Division

102 CCC *See Catechism of the Catholic Church 253, 791 for further reading on chapter content.*

Chapter 12 Helping Others

The Lord loves good deeds.

Based on Psalm 11:7

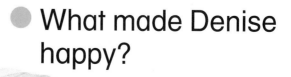Read to Me — Let's Begin

The Kindness Basket

Denise was sick. She missed a lot of school. Her classmates wanted to cheer her up. They made cards for her. They made her favorite cookies. They put the things in a basket. Miss Shay took the basket to Denise. Denise was happy to see the basket.

● What made Denise happy?

© Our Sunday Visitor Curriculum Division

103

The Church Serves

Miss Shay's class wanted to
show love to Denise.
Your Church family shows love
by serving others.

Matthew 25:35–36

 Read to Me

Ways to Serve

Feed people who are
    hungry and thirsty.
Give clothes to people
    who need them.
Be friendly to new people.
Based on Matthew 25:35–36

❓ **How can you serve?**

You Can Serve

You show love when you serve others.
You can choose different ways to serve.

Activity

Pretend you are walking to church with a friend and your family.

Act out what you see on the way. Show how you can serve others.

Choosing to Serve

Everyone can serve in some way. Some grownups serve others every day.

Activity

Tell how each person in the picture serves others.

Asking Prayer

Leader: Dear Jesus, help us serve people.

All: **Help us follow you.**

Leader: Help us be kind to each other.

All: **Help us follow you.**

Leader: Help us share with one another.

All: **Help us follow you. Amen.**

Sing together.

I am the Church!
    You are the Church!
We are the Church together.
All who follow Jesus,
    all around the world!
Yes, we're the Church together.

We Are the Church

107

Family Faith

Catholics Believe

Dear Family,
In Chapter 12, the children learned that Jesus wants us to serve by feeding the hungry, giving drinks to the thirsty, and giving clothing to the needy. The children also learned that members of the Church family serve in different ways.

SCRIPTURE

Read Matthew 25:35–36 together with your child.

GO online www.osvcurriculum.com
For weekly scripture readings and seasonal resources

Family Project

Serve Your Community Gather toys and clothes that your child has outgrown. Talk with your child about how these items are no longer useful to him or her. Explain that these clothes and toys would be useful to children who need them. With your child, take the items to a Saint Vincent de Paul Center or another organization that will distribute them to the needy. Praise your child's service to others.

People of Faith

With the Holy Spirit's help, Saint Philip told people how to follow Jesus.

**Saint Philip ▶
the Apostle,
first Century**

Family Prayer

Saint Philip, you told people how to follow Jesus. Help us know how to follow Jesus, too. Amen.

© Our Sunday Visitor Curriculum Division

CCC *See Catechism of the Catholic Church 910, 2447 for further reading on chapter content.*

Scripture Story

Paul's Message

(Colossians 1:24–25; 3:2, 8–11, 13–17)

Sing and pray to God.

Most of all, thank God for his love.

Do these things in Jesus' name.

That is what Paul told us to do.

Draw yourself following Paul's advice.

Family Note: In class your child has learned that members of the Church are to live good lives. After reading this Scripture Story together, ask your child to tell you some of Saint Paul's suggestions for living good lives. The next time you attend Mass together, listen for more advice on living good lives.

Long ago, a man named Paul
loved God.
Paul taught about Jesus.
He traveled to many places
to teach.

2

Jesus wants us to live in peace.
Try to keep Jesus' peace in
your heart.
Teach other people about Jesus.

7

Paul wrote letters to the people he had taught.

He told them how to behave.

We still read his letters today.

They are part of the Bible.

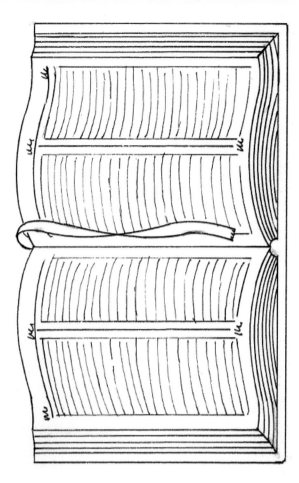

Color the Bible.

3

Forgive each other.

Remember, Jesus forgave people who hurt him.

That is why you must forgive people who hurt you.

6

III

This is what Paul wrote to some Christians in a place called Colossae.

I send you happiness from God the Father.

Jesus is with everyone who is in the Church.

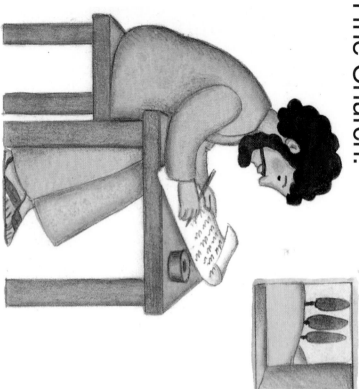

4

Think about what God wants you to do.

Be nice to everyone.

Don't be angry or tell lies.

Remember that Jesus loves everyone.

5

You Show Love

 The Lord loves justice and right.

Psalm 33:5

 Let's Begin

The Big Circle

Sara helped Troy by opening the door for him.

Troy picked Pam's paper up from the floor.

Pam shared her snack with Mary Joy.

Then Mary Joy made Sara a special toy.

What a loving group!

● What happens when one person is kind to another?

Be Kind

The children in the classroom were kind to one another.

Jesus teaches you to be kind.

He wants you to show love.

John 15:9, 12

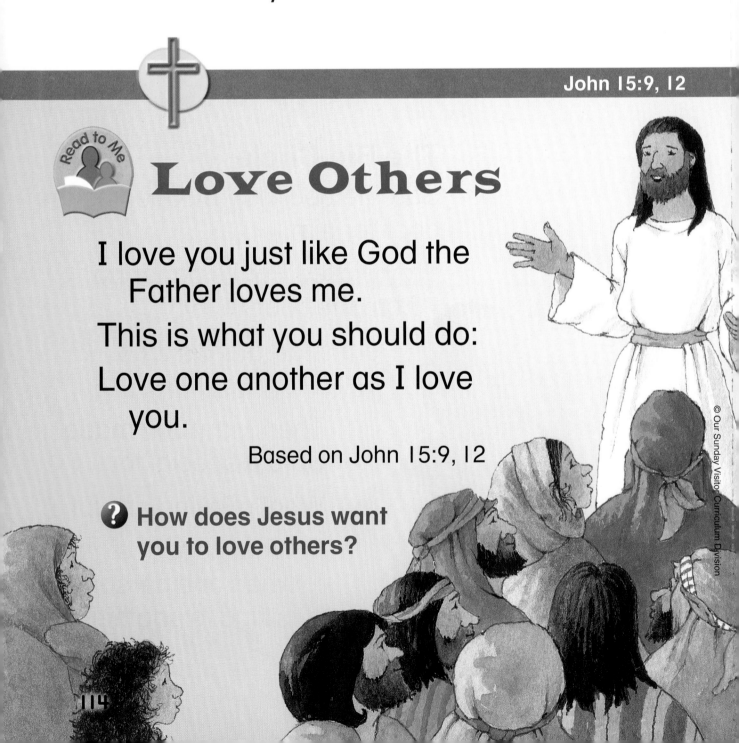

Read to Me

Love Others

I love you just like God the Father loves me.
This is what you should do:
Love one another as I love you.

Based on John 15:9, 12

❓ **How does Jesus want you to love others?**

Love as Jesus Loves

Jesus showed love in many ways.
He obeyed his parents.
He prayed to God the Father.
He visited the sick.

Activity

Draw a ♡ around the pictures that show love.

Love Others

When you love other people, you do good things for them. This makes them happy. It makes you happy, too.

Activity

✏️ Listen to the beginning of each rhyme. Help your teacher finish the rhyme. Then connect the rhyme with its picture.

Taylor did not have a treat, so John gave her a peach to _____.

Molly had a sad, sad, look, so Seamus read her favorite _____.

Prayer of Praise

Leader: Jesus, you give us a wonderful gift. You give us your love. You show us how to love and forgive others. We praise you and love you when we love others.

All: **Amen.**

Sing together.

Love one another,
Love one another,
as I have loved you.

Care for each other,
Care for each other,
as I care for you.

Love One Another

Family Faith

◎ Catholics Believe

Dear Family,

In Chapter 13, the children learned that Jesus wants them to love others as he loves them. They talked about loving actions and how these actions make people happy.

✝ SCRIPTURE

Read John 15:9,12 together with your child.

GO online **www.osvcurriculum.com**
For weekly scripture readings and seasonal resources

Family Project

Make a Star Chart Encourage loving actions by making a chart. "Catch" your child being good. Put a gold star on the chart every time he or she is kind, helpful, patient, generous, etc. Praise your child when the chart is full of stars.

People of Faith

Moses was a great leader long before Jesus was born. God chose Moses to be a leader of his people. Moses helped God's people.

Moses, 12th Century B.C. ▶

🙌 Family Prayer

Almighty God, help us follow your rules for us. Help us show love and care to others. Amen.

CCC *See Catechism of the Catholic Church 1825 for further reading on chapter content.*

Good Choices

The law of the Lord is perfect.

Psalm 19:8

Read to Me

Let's Begin

Tanya's Choice

Tanya is in a big hurry.

She wants to play with her friend George.

Tanya must cross the street.

She can play with George sooner if she crosses in the middle of the block.

What should Tanya do?

● What other rules help keep you safe?

Help with Choices

You make choices every day.
Parents help you make choices.
Teachers help you make choices.
God the Holy Spirit helps you, too.

Activity

Circle the picture with the choice the child should make.

God's Rules

Jesus reminded his followers about God's rules.

Matthew 19:18–19

Jesus Teaches

Don't hurt anyone.

Take care of your body.

Don't take other people's things.

Tell the truth.

Obey your father and mother.

Love others as you love yourself.

Based on Matthew 19:18–19

❓ **What are some ways you can follow God's rules?**

God's Rules Help

God's rules help you make good choices.

God's rules help you love yourself and others.

God's rules are called the Ten Commandments.

Activity

Draw yourself making a good choice.

Thanking Prayer

Leader: Jesus, you show us how to help others.

All: **You show us how to help others.**

Leader: You teach us about God's rules.

All: **You teach us about God's rules.**

Leader: Thank you for your help!

All: **Thank you for your help! Amen.**

 **Sing together.**

Love one another,
Love one another,
as I have loved you.

Care for each other,
Care for each other,
as I care for you.

Love One Another

Family Faith

Catholics Believe

Dear Family,

In Chapter 14, the children learned that parents, teachers, and God help them make good choices. The children also learned about the Ten Commandments.

 SCRIPTURE

Read Matthew 19:18–19 together with your child.

GO online www.osvcurriculum.com
For weekly scripture readings and seasonal resources

Family Project

Making Good Choices
Make an artistic reminder of the steps to making good choices. On a sheet of paper, draw a stoplight. In the top light, write STOP; in the middle light, write THINK; in the bottom light, write CHOOSE. Have your child color each part of the light with the proper color. Reinforce the ideas of stopping before making choices, thinking about rules that will help make the choices, and choosing wisely.

People of Faith

God gave the Ten Commandments to Moses. The Ten Commandments help people know how to show love to God and other people.

Moses, 12th Century B.C. ▶

Family Prayer

God our Father, thank you for the rules you gave to Moses. Help us follow your rules and show love for others. Amen.

Chapter 15 Forgive Others

God shows them the way to choose.

Based on Psalm 25:12

 Let's Begin

Fixing Things

Lisa was worried. "I fell and tore my new dress," she said.

Lisa's mother said, "We can fix it. You can help me. Bring me my sewing box, please."

● What is Lisa doing in the picture?

Help for Hurts

Sometimes friendships are hurt.
You can make a friendship better.
You can use words to help it.
You can do things to help it.

Activity

Connect the pictures to show how to fix a friendship.

Forgive One Another

What should you do if someone is mean to you?

You should forgive that person.

God wants us to forgive others.

Matthew 18:21–22

Forgiveness

Peter asked Jesus how many times he should forgive someone.

"Must I forgive him seven times?" Peter asked.

"No, you must forgive him many more times than that," Jesus said.

Based on Matthew 18:21–22

❓ **What does Jesus say about forgiveness?**

Special Signs

Special words can help make things better with family or friends.

"I am sorry."

"I forgive you."

Special signs can help you make things better, too.

Smile

High-five

Hug

Kiss

❓ **When do you use these signs?**

Forgiving Prayer

Leader: Dear God, sometimes I hurt others.

All: **Help me live in love.**

Leader: Help me show that I am sorry.

All: **Help me live in love.**

Leader: Sometimes others hurt me.

All: **Help me live in love.**

Leader: Help me show forgiveness.

All: **Help me live in love. Amen.**

Sing together.

Love one another,
Love one another,
as I have loved you.

Care for each other,
Care for each other,
as I care for you.

Love One Another

Family Faith

 Catholics Believe

Dear Family,

In Chapter 15, the children learned that friendships can be made better. They heard the Bible story about forgiving others. They also learned words and gestures that show sorrow and forgiveness.

 SCRIPTURE

Read together Matthew 18:21–22 with your child.

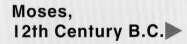 **www.osvcurriculum.com**
For weekly scripture readings and seasonal resources

Family Project

Showing Forgiveness Practice words and ways of repairing hurt relationships. Use hugs, kisses, handshakes, and phrases such as "I forgive you" to show forgiveness. Point out that the Sign of Peace exchanged at Mass shows that we are at peace with one another. Make this part of the Mass more meaningful by adding personal comments of sorrow and forgiveness.

People of Faith

Moses forgave his friends who forgot to love God and others.

**Moses,
12th Century B.C.** ▶

 Family Prayer

God our Father, help us forgive other people when they hurt us. Help us show sorrow when we hurt others. Amen.

Scripture Story

Jesus and Zacchaeus

(Luke 19:1–10)

Family Note: In class your child has learned that God wants us to make loving choices and to ask forgiveness when we have hurt others. After reading this Scripture Story together, talk about how Zacchaeus changed because of Jesus. The next time you recognize that your child is trying hard to be a better person, praise his or her actions.

Jesus smiled. He said to Zacchaeus, "You are trying to be a better person.

Good for you! You are a special child of God!"

Color in Jesus and Zacchaeus.

8

Jesus was traveling with his friends.

They came to a town.

The people in the town were excited about seeing Jesus.

They gathered in a big crowd.

Zacchaeus knew what they were saying.

He told Jesus, "I will give away half of what I own.

I will pay back the people who I cheated.

I will give them more than I took from them."

A man named Zacchaeus lived in the town.

He was very short.

He could not see Jesus because everyone else was so tall.

3

The people in the town were surprised.

They said, "Why does Jesus want Zacchaeus for a friend? We know that he cheats people."

6

Zacchaeus had an idea.
He would climb a tree!
Then he could see Jesus
and hear him.

Jesus looked up. He saw
Zacchaeus.

He said, "Zacchaeus,
come down.

I want to eat at your
house today."

For with you is the fountain of life.

Psalm 36:10

Read to Me — Let's Begin —

Signs Everywhere

We see signs everywhere we go.

Signs give us information.

They give us directions.

Signs can also tell us about love.

● What does this sign mean? What other signs do you know about?

Sunday Visitor Curriculum Di...

Jesus' Signs

The world is full of signs.

Jesus used signs to teach people.

He used signs to show people God's love.

The Church family uses the signs Jesus used.

Water

Light

Food

❓ **When does the Church family use these signs?**

Blessing Food

Many people were listening to Jesus. They were hungry.

A boy had brought some bread and fish.

This wasn't enough food for so many! Jesus blessed the boy's food.

Jesus' friends shared the food with everyone. They all had more than enough to eat.

Based on John 6:1–13

❓ What did Jesus do?

137

Signs of God's Love

Jesus blessed the bread and fish.

The blessing and the food were signs of God's love.

Activity

Your teacher will give you a clue.

Find the sign that fits the clue.

Cover the sign with a marker.

Thanking Prayer

Leader: God our Father, you have given us many signs of your love. We have our beautiful world. We have our friends and families. These are wonderful signs. But the best sign of your love is your Son, Jesus. Thank you for all of your love.

All: Amen.

Sing together.

The Lord has done great
   things for us;
We are filled with joy,
We are filled with joy.

Psalm 126:
The Lord Has Done
Great Things

Family Faith

Catholics Believe

Dear Family,

In Chapter 16, the children learned that special signs tell about God's love for us. Jesus used signs when he taught people. They also reviewed some of the signs of God's love that they have learned about this year.

SCRIPTURE

Read Mark 6:34–42 together with your child.

GO online www.osvcurriculum.com
For weekly scripture readings and seasonal resources

Family Project

Signs of Love Send a sign of love to a friend or family member who is far away. Take your child to a local post office, and allow him or her to purchase a postcard. Help your child write a message of love on the card and address it. With your child, mail the card. Talk about how the message will brighten the day of the receiver. Relate this happiness to the happiness we receive from God's messages of love to us in the Bible.

People of Faith

John the Baptist was Jesus' cousin. God sent John as a sign of love to his parents and to all the people that he met.

Saint John ▶ the Baptist, 1 B.C.–32 A.D.

Family Prayer

God our Father, thank you for your signs of love to us. Help us see and appreciate them. Amen.

© Our Sunday Visitor Curriculum Division

Chapter 17

Baptism

To safe waters you lead me.

Psalm 23:2

Read to Me

Let's Begin

A Riddle

What is in the rain but not in a chain?

What is in a creek but not in a cheek?

What is in a tear but not in a cheer?

● Where else can you find water?

Life from Water

Everything needs water to live.
You drink water.
People wash and cook with water.
Some animals live in water.

❓ **How else do you use water?**

Activity

Find and color all the things
that use water.

A Sign of Love

Jesus' followers used water as a sign of God's life and love.

They used water to baptize new Church members.

A New Member

Philip told a young man about Jesus.

The young man said, "I want to follow Jesus. Please baptize me."

The young man went into the water and was baptized. He was very happy.

Based on Acts 8:35–40

❓ **Why was the man happy?**

A Special Celebration

Baptism is a special Church celebration.

At Baptism, a person becomes a member of the Church.

Like Philip, the priest uses water to baptize.

The priest also says special words.

Then the person belongs to the Church family.

❓ What do you know about your Baptism?

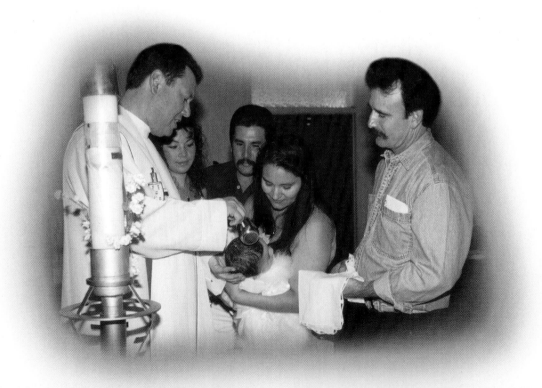

Prayer of Praise

Leader: Water is in all living things.

All:　　**We praise you for water.**

Leader: Water helps plants grow.

All:　　**We praise you for water.**

Leader: Water takes away our thirst.

All:　　**We praise you for water.**

Leader: Water welcomed us into your Church.

All:　　**We praise you for water. Amen.**

Sing together.

The Lord has done great things for us;

We are filled with joy,

We are filled with joy.

Psalm 126: The Lord
Has Done Great Things

Catholics Believe

Dear Family,

In Chapter 17, the children learned that water is a sign of God's life and love. The Church uses water to baptize new members. The children also learned that they became members of the Church family at Baptism.

SCRIPTURE

Read Acts 8:35–40 together with your child.

 www.osvcurriculum.com
For weekly scripture readings and seasonal resources

Family Project

Share a Baptism Story Tell your child about his or her Baptism. Tell how you selected his or her godparents and how you felt as your child was being baptized. If you have pictures or a videotape of the event, share them with your child. The next time you visit your parish church, remind your child to bless himself or herself with holy water. Point out that these blessings recall our Baptism.

People of Faith

John told people how to love God. He baptized many people in the Jordan River.

Saint John the Baptist, I B.C.–32 A.D.

Family Prayer

Dear God, thank you for the sacrament of Baptism. Help us be good members of your Church family. Amen.

© Our Sunday Visitor Curriculum Division

Eucharist

 You set a table before me.

Psalm 23:5

Read to Me

Let's Begin

Bread

Brown toast for breakfast,
bagels for lunch,
shortbread for snack.

Flat pitas for wrapping,
bent croissants for dipping,
square matzo for munching.

Bread is shared
in near and far places.
It gives us full stomachs
and happy faces.

● Why do you eat
bread?

© Our Sunday Visitor Curriculum Division

147

A Sign of Life

Jesus ate bread, too.
He shared bread with his friends.

Mark 14:22–24

The Last Supper

Jesus and his friends were sharing
a special supper.

Bread and wine were on the table.

Jesus blessed the bread and gave
it to his friends.

He said, "This is my body."

Then Jesus gave thanks over the
wine and shared it.

He said, "This is my blood."

Based on Mark 14:22–24

❓ **When does the
Church say these
words of Jesus?**

The Mass

The Church remembers the Last Supper at each Mass.

At Mass you hear readings from the Bible.

Everyone gathered gives thanks and praise to God.

The priest says and does what Jesus did at the Last Supper.

Activity

Look at the Mass pictures. Describe what is taking place in each.

149

Really Jesus

The blessed Bread and Wine at Mass are called the Holy Eucharist.

The blessed Bread and Wine are really Jesus' Body and Blood.

Jesus told his friends that he is the Bread of Life.

Sharing the Eucharist brings Church members closer to Jesus.

Activity

Draw a picture of yourself in Church.

Pray with God's Word

Leader: Let us listen to God's word from the Bible.

Read Mark 14:22–24.

The word of the Lord.

All: **Thanks be to God.**

Sing together.

The Lord has done great things for us;
We are filled with joy,
We are filled with joy.

Psalm 126: The Lord Has
Done Great Things

Family Faith

 ## Catholics Believe

Dear Family,

In Chapter 18, the children learned that at the Last Supper, Jesus celebrated the first Eucharist. He changed bread and wine into his Body and Blood. At Mass, Jesus is again with us in the Holy Eucharist.

 ## SCRIPTURE

Read Mark 14:22–24 together with your child.

 www.osvcurriculum.com
For weekly scripture readings and seasonal resources

Family Project

Baking Bread Find a simple recipe for bread, assemble the ingredients, and have your child help you measure, mix, and knead the dough. As the bread bakes, talk about how people all over the world eat some form of bread. Before eating your bread, bless it and thank God for this gift.

People of Faith

Saint John the Baptist told people about Jesus before he baptized them.

Saint John ▶ the Baptist, 1 B.C.–32 A.D.

 ## Family Prayer

Saint John the Baptist, you shared stories about Jesus and led others to God. Pray for us that we may be like you. Amen.

Scripture Story
The Last Supper
(Mark 14:22–26)

At Mass, the bread and wine become Jesus. We remember him as he asked us to.

Family Note: In class your child has learned that bread and wine are signs of God's love. After reading this Scripture Story together, ask your child to tell you what Jesus said about his Body and Blood. The next time you attend Mass with your child, point out that Jesus is really present in the bread (host) and the wine of the Eucharist.

8

Jesus and his friends had a very special dinner. We call it the Last Supper.

Jesus said, "This is my Blood. When you drink, remember me."

© Our Sunday Visitor Curriculum Division

154

This was the last meal Jesus
would eat with his friends.
They had bread and wine.

3

Then Jesus gave thanks over
the wine.

6

Jesus blessed the bread and shared it.

Jesus said, "This is my Body."

4

5

Being with God

 The Lord's throne is in heaven.

Psalm 11:4

Let's Begin

God's House

God's house is a happy place
Where you will not see a sad face.
A place so shiny and so bright
Because it's filled with holy light.
No need to be sad or to cry
Because God's love is so nearby.

● What sort of place does this poem describe?

A Perfect Place

Heaven is where God is.

God wants all of his children to be with him in heaven.

Everything is perfect in heaven.

Everyone is happy in heaven.

In heaven no one gets sick.

In heaven no one is sad.

In heaven no one gets hurt.

What Is Heaven Like?

God has wonderful things planned for the people who love him.

Heaven is better than anything that anyone has ever seen or heard.

Based on I Corinthians 2:9

❓ What do you think will be the best thing about heaven?

In God's Home

Jesus told us about heaven, too.

Jesus said, "Heaven is like a huge house.

God's house has many rooms.

I will make a place for you there."

Based on John 14:1–31

Activity

Draw yourself in God's house.

Prayer of Praise

Leader: God our Father, we love you.

All: **Alleluia!**

Leader: Thank you for making heaven.

All: **Alleluia!**

Leader: We want to be with you and Jesus there someday.

All: **Alleluia! Amen.**

Sing together.

We are walking in the light,
in the light,
in the light.
We are walking in the light,
in the light of God.

We Are Walking in the Light

Catholics Believe

Dear Family,
In Chapter 19, the children discussed heaven in simple terms. They learned that heaven is a perfect place. Jesus is preparing a home for us there.

SCRIPTURE

Read I Corinthians 2:9 together with your child.

GO online **www.osvcurriculum.com**
For weekly scripture readings and seasonal resources

Family Project

Draw Together With your child, draw a picture of what you think heaven looks like. Draw Jesus, God the Father, the Holy Spirit, patron saints, relatives, and others who you think are in heaven. Everyone should look happy. Talk about how we love and serve God on earth so that we can join God in heaven someday.

People of Faith

When Thérèse was very young, she wanted to serve God. She gave money to the poor because she worried about them. When she was fifteen years old, she chose to become a nun.

Saint Thérèse ▶ of Lisieux, 1873–1897

Family Prayer

Loving God, help us learn about you and serve you well. Help us love others as you have loved us. Amen.

© Our Sunday Visitor Curriculum Division

Chapter 20 Be Like God

 Continue your kindness toward your friends.

Psalm 36:11

 **Read to Me**

Let's Begin

Little Things

"What makes God happy?" Jerry asked.

"God is happy with little things," his mother said.

"What kind of little things?" His mother thought.

"Be nice to other people.

Cheer up people who are sad.

Help at home and school.

Making other people happy makes God happy."

● What is a little thing you can do at home or school?

163

Holy People

God wants everyone to be good and happy.
Saints are friends of God and holy followers of Jesus.
Each day they helped people.
Each day they prayed.
Now they are in heaven.

Activity

Write the name of your favorite saint on the line below.

Saint

_____

- -

_____

pray for us.

Saints

Saint Paul told us how to be like the saints.

Ephesians 5:1–2, 7–10

Live in the Light

Be like God, and live with love.

Stay in God's light because it will make you good.

God's light will make you truthful.

Find out what pleases God, and then do it.

Based on Ephesians 5:1–2, 7–10

How can you find out what pleases God?

165

As You Grow

God loves the small things you do
for him now.
You will not always be small.
You will grow up someday.
God will love what you do then, too.

Activity

Connect each picture of a child
with the picture of an adult who is
helping people in a similar way.

166

Prayer for Help

Leader: Thank you, God, for little things.

All: **Thank you, God, for little things.**

Leader: Help us help others in little ways.

All: **Help us help others in little ways.**

Leader: Help us stay in your light.

All: **Help us stay in your light. Amen.**

Sing together.

We are walking in the light,
in the light,
in the light.
We are walking in the light,
in the light of God.

We Are Walking in the Light

Family Faith

Catholics Believe

Dear Family,

In Chapter 20, the children learned that God is pleased with little acts of kindness. They learned that saints are holy people in heaven. Children learned that as they grow, they will do many things for God.

SCRIPTURE

Read Ephesians 5:1–2, 7–10 together with your child.

GO online www.osvcurriculum.com
For weekly scripture readings and seasonal resources

Family Project

Make a Chart This week, emphasize the small jobs that your child does to help in your household. To help your child keep up with chores without being reminded, make a simple job chart. Have your child use stickers or make check marks to show that a job is completed. Review the chart regularly, and praise your child's contributions to family work. Point out that even little jobs, done well, please God and help the family.

My Jobs	🧹	🧦
Sunday		✓
Monday	★	
Tuesday		
Wednesday	✓	★
Thursday		♥
Friday		
Saturday		

People of Faith

Thérèse wrote about serving God in little ways. Even when she was sick, she trusted God and loved him very much.

Saint Thérèse ▶ of Lisieux, 1873–1897

Family Prayer

Saint Thérèse, help us be like you. Help us do little things for God. Amen.

Chapter 21 Praise God

I will praise your name forever.

Psalm 145:2

Let's Begin

Celebrate, Celebrate

The year is ending.

You have learned so much this year!

You have learned a lot about God.

● Tell one thing you learned about God.

Thanks and Praise

Thank God for what you learned.

You can thank God by praising him.

You can praise God in the morning.

You can praise God in the evening.

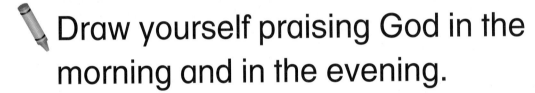

Draw yourself praising God in the morning and in the evening.

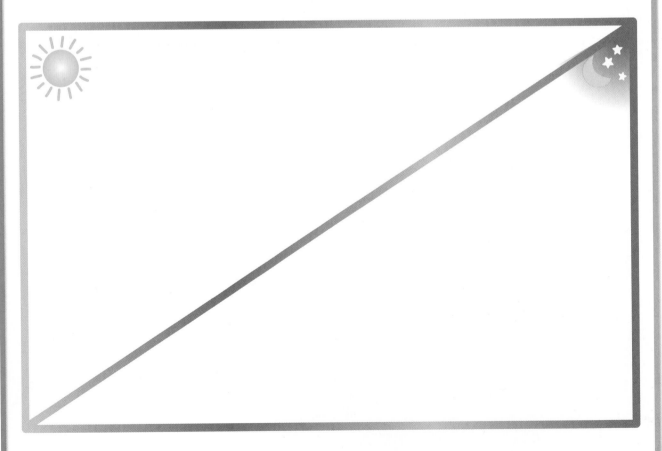

 Read to Me

Ways to Praise

Praise God in heaven.

Praise him with blasts of the horn,

Praise him with harp and lyre,

Praise him with tambourines and dancing.

Praise him with flutes and strings.

Praise him with cymbals.

Based on Psalm 150:1, 3–5

❓ How can you praise God?

Praising and Loving

God will always love you.

God gave you the world because he loves you.

God wants you to love the world.

Loving others and the world is a way to praise God.

Prayer of Praise

Leader: We praise you God the Father.

All: **We praise you God the Father.**

Leader: We praise you God the Son.

All: **We praise you God the Son.**

Leader: We praise you God the Holy Spirit.

All: **We praise you God the Holy Spirit.**

 **Sing together.**

We are walking in the light,
in the light,
in the light.
We are walking in the light,
in the light of God.

We Are Walking in the Light

Family Faith

Catholics Believe

Dear Family,

In Chapter 21, the children celebrated the end of the year. They reviewed key ideas from the year. They talked about praising God with music and prayer.

 ## SCRIPTURE

Read Psalm 150:1, 3–5 together with your child.

GO online www.osvcurriculum.com
For weekly scripture readings and seasonal resources

Family Project

Remember to Pray Make a door hanger that will help your child remember to pray throughout the summer. Cut a sheet of paper or poster board about 4" x 11". Cut a hole so that it can slip over a doorknob, or use yarn to make a loop for hanging. Write "Remember to pray!" on the hanger. Have your child decorate the remaining space and hang it on his or her bedroom door or other frequently used door.

People of Faith

Thérèse taught other sisters about God. She also wrote a book. People still read her book to learn how to serve God and other people.

Saint Thérèse of Lisieux, 1873–1897

Family Prayer

Almighty God, we love you. We praise you for what you have done for us. Thank you for our world. Amen.

Scripture Story

Easter

(Mark 15:1–16:6; John 20:11–16)

Family Note: In class your child has learned that Jesus died to save us. After reading this Scripture Story together, talk about how Jesus rose from the dead, met with his friends, and later returned to heaven to be with the Father. Then pray the Lord's Prayer together.

Jesus told Mary, "Tell my friends that I have new life from God the Father.

I will visit them soon!"

We celebrate Jesus' new life on Easter.

8

175

Many people did not like what
Jesus was teaching.
They took him to their leaders.
The leaders said that Jesus
should die.

2

© Our Sunday Visitor Curriculum Division

Then Mary looked up.
Jesus was right in front of her!
Mary was very happy!

7

176

Jesus died on the cross.

He prayed for us while he was on the cross.

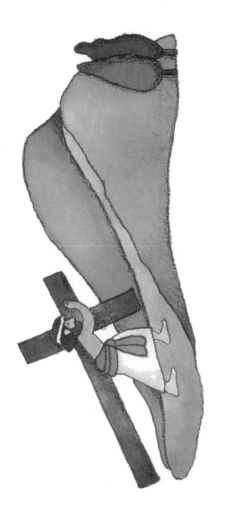

3

Mary Magdalene was one of the women at the tomb.

She was crying outside the tomb.

Someone asked her why she was sad.

She said, "I don't know where Jesus is."

6

Jesus' friends took his body.
They put it into a tomb that was cut into a rock.

They closed the tomb with a big rock.

All of Jesus' friends were very sad.

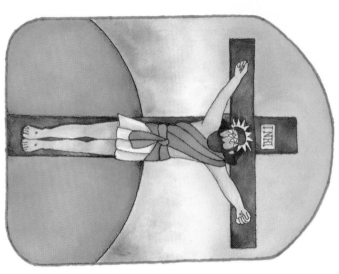

4

The next Sunday, some women went back to Jesus' tomb.

The rock was rolled back.

An angel was inside the tomb.

The angel said, "Jesus was raised from the dead! He is not here!"

5

Catholic Prayers

The Church Year

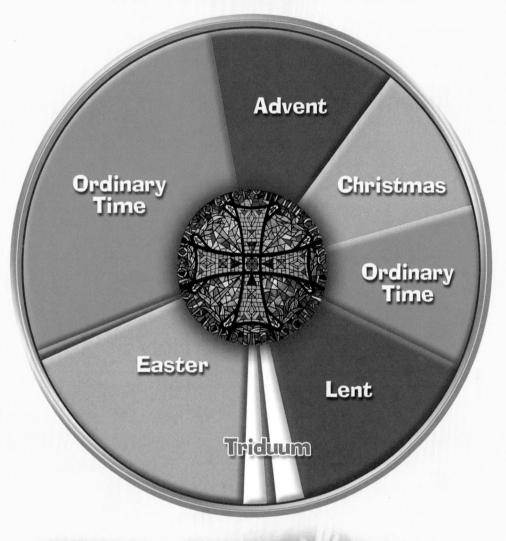

Advent

Christmas

Ordinary Time

Ordinary Time

Lent

Easter

Triduum

The Sign of the Cross

In the name of the Father,
and of the Son,
and of the Holy Spirit.
Amen.

In the name of the Father,

1

and of the Son,

2

and of the Holy Spirit.

3

4

Amen.

5

Glory to the Father

Glory to the Father,
and to the Son,
and to the Holy Spirit:
as it was in the beginning,
is now,
and will be forever. Amen.

The Lord's Prayer

Our Father, who art in heaven,
hallowed be thy name;
thy kingdom come;
thy will be done on earth as it is in heaven.
Give us this day our daily bread;
and forgive us our trespasses
as we forgive those who trespass against us;
and lead us not into temptation,
but deliver us from evil.
Amen.

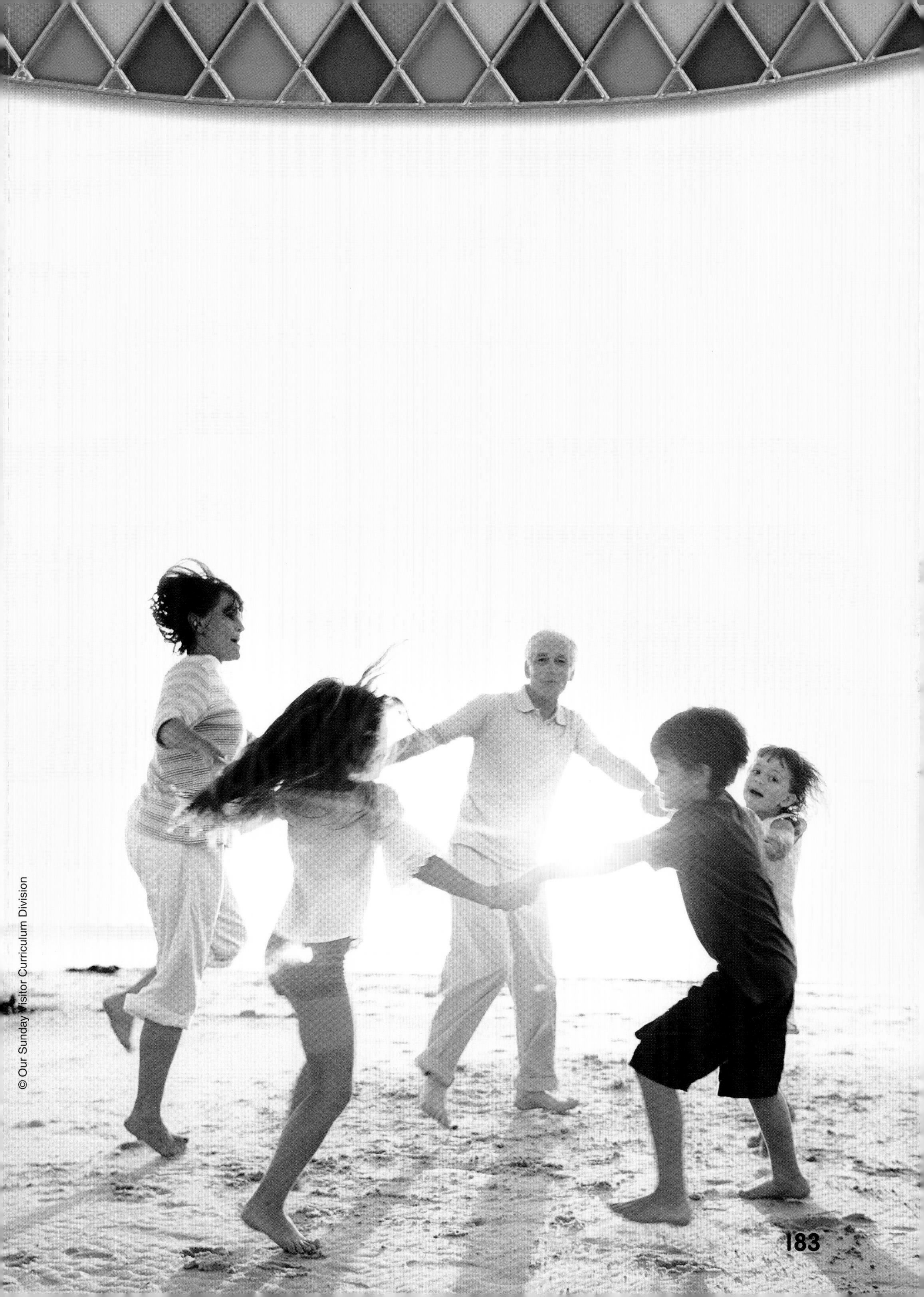

Hail Mary

Hail Mary, full of grace,
the Lord is with you!
Blessed are you among women,
and blessed is the fruit of your
womb, Jesus.
Holy Mary, Mother of God,
pray for us sinners,
now and at the hour of our death.
Amen.

185

Blessing Before Meals

Bless us, O Lord,
and these your gifts,
which we are about to receive
from your goodness.
Through Christ our Lord. Amen.

Thanksgiving After Meals

We give you thanks for all your gifts,
 almighty God,
living and reigning now and forever.
Amen.

Words of Faith

A is for an angel,
a messenger of God.

B is for Bible,
the Church's holy book.

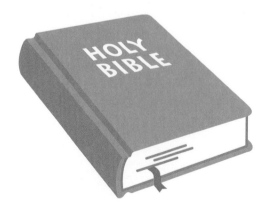

C is for Church,
our family of faith.

D is for day;
we thank God each day
for all creation.

E is for Eucharist,
the Church's holy meal.

F is for forgiveness,
a sign of God's love.

190

G is for God,
who made us and loves us.

H is for the Holy Spirit,
who helps Jesus' friends
and followers.

I is for imitate,
to act more like Jesus.

J is for Jesus,
the Son of God, who
shares his life with us.

K is for the three kings,
who visited the baby Jesus.

L is for love,
God's love and our
love for others.

M is for Mary,
the Mother of Jesus.

N is for Noah,
who took care of
God's creatures.

O is for obey,
to listen to God
and our parents.

P is for prayer,
talking and listening
to God.

Q is for questions
we ask about God's world.

R is for the rainbow
Noah saw in the sky
after the flood.

S is for saints,
God's friends who show us
how to follow Jesus.

T is for the Trinity:
God the Father, God the Son,
and God the Holy Spirit.

U is for up and down and all around; God is with us everywhere.

V is for visit, when the angel visited Mary to tell her about Jesus.

W is for our world, where all people are God's children.

X looks like a cross, the sign of Jesus.

Y is for "yes";
your family said "yes" to God
for you when you were baptized.

Z is for zebras
and all the other creatures
God made with love.